W9-CNO-397

PLANETARY
EXPLORATION

PLUTO
AND OTHER DWARF PLANETS

SHALINI SAXENA

Britannica®
Educational Publishing

IN ASSOCIATION WITH

ROSEN
EDUCATIONAL SERVICES

Published in 2017 by Britannica Educational Publishing (a trademark of Encyclopædia Britannica, Inc.) in association with The Rosen Publishing Group, Inc.
29 East 21st Street, New York, NY 10010

Distributed exclusively by Rosen Publishing.
To see additional Britannica Educational Publishing titles, go to rosenpublishing.com.

First Edition

Britannica Educational Publishing
J.E. Luebering: Executive Director, Core Editorial
Mary Rose McCudden: Editor, Britannica Student Encyclopedia

Rosen Publishing
Amelie von Zumbusch: Editor
Nelson Sá: Art Director
Michael Moy: Designer
Cindy Reiman: Photography Manager

Library of Congress Cataloging-in-Publication Data

Names: Saxena, Shalini, 1982– author.
Title: Pluto and other dwarf planets / Shalini Saxena.
Description: First edition. | New York : Britannica Educational Publishing in association with Rosen Educational Services, 2017. | Series: Planetary exploration | Audience: Grades 1 to 4. | Includes bibliographical references and index.
Identifiers: LCCN 2016024229| ISBN 9781508104230 (library bound) | ISBN 9781508104247 (pbk.) | ISBN 9781508103110 (6-pack)
Subjects: LCSH: Dwarf planets—Juvenile literature. | Pluto (Dwarf planet)—Juvenile literature. | Kuiper Belt—Juvenile literature. | Outer space—Exploration—Juvenile literature.
Classification: LCC QB698 .S29 2017 | DDC 523.49/22—dc23
LC record available at https://lccn.loc.gov/2016024229

Manufactured in China

CONTENTS

WHAT IS A DWARF PLANET?

In 1930, an American astronomer named Clyde Tombaugh noticed something unusual while looking through a telescope. He thought it was a new planet, and other scientists agreed. The scientists named it Pluto. It was considered the smallest planet in the solar system until 2006.

In 2006, a group of astronomers decided that the definition of "planet" did not apply to Pluto. It is now considered a dwarf planet. Like planets, dwarf planets are large, roundish objects that orbit, or travel

Clyde Tombaugh took this photograph of Pluto, shown with an arrow, in 1930.

around, the sun or other stars. Both planets and dwarf planets have **gravity**. The gravity of planets is strong enough to clear their orbits of smaller objects by attracting the objects to them. The gravity of dwarf planets is weaker.

Pluto was one of the names ancient Romans used for their god of the underworld.

Charon (*left*) is one of the five known moons of the dwarf planet Pluto (*right*).

Dwarf planets can have **satellites**, such as moons, like planets do. They can spin around an axis like planets do, too.

Dwarf planets are also similar to asteroids. These are small, rocky bodies that orbit the sun. Asteroids are considered minor planets, but they are not always big or round enough to be dwarf planets.

There are five known dwarf planets in our solar system: Pluto, Eris, Ceres, Makemake, and Haumea. Scientists believe there are many more, although they do not always

VOCABULARY

Satellites are small objects that orbit larger objects in space. They can be natural or made by humans.

agree on what counts as a dwarf planet. In 2008, scientists came up with a new subcategory of dwarf planets: plutoids. A plutoid is a dwarf planet whose orbit takes it farther from the sun than the planet Neptune. Pluto, Makemake, Haumea, and Eris are dwarf planets and also plutoids. Ceres, which orbits much closer to the sun, is a dwarf planet but not a plutoid.

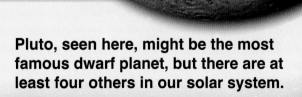

Pluto, seen here, might be the most famous dwarf planet, but there are at least four others in our solar system.

THE KUIPER BELT

The Kuiper belt lies just outside Neptune's orbit. It has millions of icy bodies orbiting the sun. Most of these are small, but some are large enough to be considered dwarf planets. The dwarf planets Pluto, Eris, Makemake, and Haumea are all in the Kuiper belt.

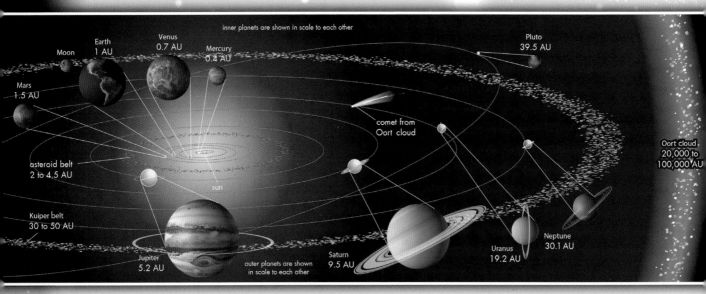

inner planets are shown in scale to each other

Earth 1 AU
Moon
Venus 0.7 AU
Mercury 0.4 AU
Mars 1.5 AU
Pluto 39.5 AU
Oort cloud 20,000 to 100,000 AU
asteroid belt 2 to 4.5 AU
comet from Oort cloud
sun
Kuiper belt 30 to 50 AU
Jupiter 5.2 AU
Saturn 9.5 AU
Uranus 19.2 AU
Neptune 30.1 AU
outer planets are shown in scale to each other

The distance between each object and the sun is shown in astronomical units (AU). One AU equals the average distance from Earth to the sun.

THINK ABOUT IT

The main asteroid belt is closer to the sun than the Kuiper belt. Why do you think the Kuiper belt has more icy comets than the asteroid belt?

Unlike the other dwarf planets, Ceres is in the main asteroid belt. Most of the solar system's asteroids are found here. The main belt lies between the orbits of Jupiter and Mars.

Uranus and Neptune are the outermost planets of our solar system. Scientists think that many of the objects in the Kuiper belt were left over from when these two planets formed. The Kuiper belt was discovered in 1992 when astronomers found a large object orbiting beyond the orbit of Neptune. Many other large objects have since been found. By 2006 astronomers decided that Pluto should be grouped with these objects rather than with the planets.

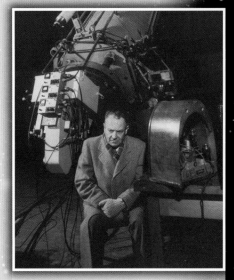

The Kuiper belt is named for the astronomer Gerard Kuiper.

PLUTO

Pluto's diameter, or the distance through its center, is about 1,430 miles (2,300 kilometers). This is less than half the diameter of the smallest planet, Mercury.

Scientists think that Pluto consists of rocky material and frozen gases. Some areas of Pluto's surface are very bright, while others are dark. The bright regions are probably due to a frozen gas called nitrogen.

Pluto is so far from the sun that it receives only a little sunlight. Scientists believe that the average temperature on its surface is about −387° F (−233° C).

When the New Horizons space probe passed by Pluto in 2015, it captured the first detailed images of the dwarf planet's icy surface.

In what ways is Pluto like a planet? In what ways is it like an asteroid? How is it different from each?

Like the planets, Pluto has two types of motion: orbit and spin. Pluto completes one orbit around the sun every 248 Earth years. That means that a year on Pluto lasts 248 Earth years. Pluto spins about its axis slowly. It completes one rotation in about 6.5 Earth days, so a Pluto day lasts about 6.5 Earth days.

Pluto's orbit is less circular than the orbits of the four outer planets, shown here in blue.

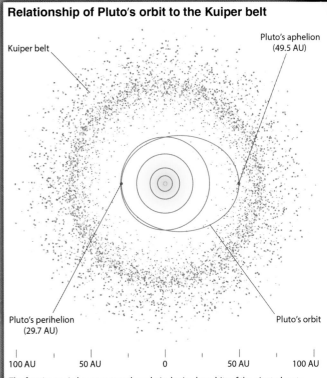

Relationship of Pluto's orbit to the Kuiper belt

Kuiper belt

Pluto's aphelion (49.5 AU)

Pluto's perihelion (29.7 AU)

Pluto's orbit

| 100 AU | 50 AU | 0 | 50 AU | 100 AU |

The four inner circles represent the relatively circular orbits of the giant planets (outward from center) Jupiter, Saturn, Uranus, and Neptune. Orbits of the inner planets are not shown.

Because Pluto is so far from Earth, it is difficult to observe with even the most powerful telescopes. Key observations have been made using instruments that orbit Earth from above its atmosphere, including the **Hubble Space Telescope**.

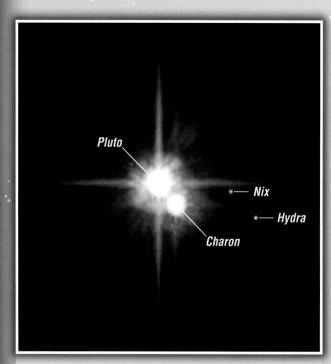

Pluto

Nix

Hydra

Charon

The Hubble Space Telescope captured this image of Pluto and three of its five moons.

Pluto has five known moons: Charon, Nix, Hydra, Kerberos, and Styx. Charon is much larger than the other four.

In 2006, the United States launched a space probe, called New Horizons, to explore Pluto. That was also the year scientists decided Pluto was a dwarf planet rather than a planet. New Horizons flew by Pluto and Charon in July

2015, investigating their atmospheres and surfaces. It observed a large heart-shaped region of ice on Pluto and discovered large chasms on Charon. It also observed mountains that might be ice volcanoes on Pluto.

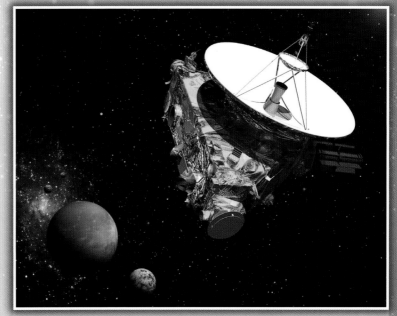

New Horizons was the first spacecraft to reach the Kuiper belt. After its nine-year journey to Pluto, it continued to explore nearby objects.

ERIS

Eris's diameter is 1,445 miles (2,326 km), making it slightly smaller than Pluto. Eris is even more remote than Pluto. On average, it is nearly 68 times farther from the sun than is Earth. Scientists calculate that it takes Eris 560 Earth years to complete one orbit around the sun.

Eris's orbit is so tilted that some scientists call it a member of the Kuiper belt's scattered disc rather than of the Kuiper belt itself. The scattered disc lies just beyond the

This photo of Eris was taken by the Hubble Space Telescope. Eris is so far from Earth that it is hard to see without special equipment.

Kuiper belt, though parts of the two overlap. Eris's surface may have white ice made of methane, a substance commonly found as a gas on Earth. Eris has one known moon, Dysnomia. It is about an eighth the size of Eris and takes about two weeks to circle the dwarf planet.

This drawing shows what Eris might look like near its surface, with the sun pictured in the distance.

Eris was discovered in 2005 by examining images that had been taken two years earlier at Palomar Observatory in southern California. The Kuiper belt object was first called 2003 UB313. It was nicknamed "Xena" and "the 10th planet" before receiving its official name in 2006. Eris was named after the goddess of disagreement or conflict in ancient Greek mythology.

The Palomar Observatory in California is the site of important developments in space science, including the discovery of Eris.

The name Eris is fitting because the discovery of the celestial object led to a great controversy in the world of planetary science. Since Eris is about the same size as Pluto, some

THINK ABOUT IT

Some scientists still think Eris, Pluto, and other bodies should be called planets. Do you agree? Why or why not?

scientists thought that it also should be considered one of the solar system's major planets. Others thought that a new classification was needed for bodies such as Pluto and Eris. Eris was declared a dwarf planet in 2006, along with Pluto.

People who felt badly about losing Pluto as a planet left notes such as these at the Smithsonian Castle in Washington, DC.

HAUMEA

Haumea is thought to be roughly three quarters the size of Pluto. Haumea is a very unusual dwarf planet. It spins on its axis much faster than any other large celestial object, completing one rotation in about four hours. Haumea's rapid rotation probably accounts for its odd shape, which is somewhat like a squashed football. Haumea is massive enough that its gravity would normally have pulled it into a rounded shape, but the pull of its remarkably fast rotation stretches it out.

The other known dwarf planets are much rounder in shape than Haumea, shown between its two moons in this drawing.

Why do you think a faster rotation, or spin, around its axis might affect the shape of Haumea?

Scientists think that most Kuiper belt objects are about half rock and half ice, but Haumea seems to be nearly all rock with a thin surface coating of ice. Astronomers think that Haumea may once have had much more ice.

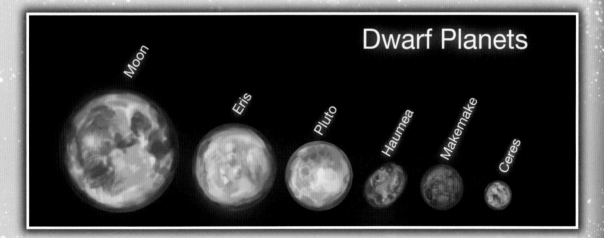

Dwarf Planets

Moon

Eris

Pluto

Haumea

Makemake

Ceres

Dwarf planets vary in size and shape. But all of the known dwarf planets in our solar system are smaller than Earth's moon.

In the distant past, a collision with another object may have knocked most of Haumea's ice off and caused it to start spinning faster. According to this theory, the knocked-off icy pieces formed Haumea's two known moons—Hi'iaka and Namaka—and several other small icy objects nearby that have orbits similar to Haumea's.

Haumea orbits the sun from an average distance of about 4 billion miles (6.5 billion km) away. It is about 43 times farther from the sun than Earth is.

Haumea's moons were named after two daughters of the goddess Haumea. Namaka is a sea goddess. The ocean is very important in Hawaiian culture.

Before Haumea got its name, it was also called "Santa." What other names might make sense for it?

It takes Haumea more than 283 Earth years to complete one orbit.

Haumea was at first known as 2003 EL61. Its discovery was announced in 2005, and in 2008 it was officially categorized as a dwarf planet and a plutoid. (A plutoid is a dwarf planet that is farther from the sun on average than Neptune is.) Haumea was named after a Hawaiian goddess of birth.

Mike Brown headed the team that discovered Eris. Both Brown's team and a team of Spanish scientists claim to have discovered Haumea.

MAKEMAKE

With a diameter of about 900 miles (1,500 km), Makemake is roughly two thirds the size of Pluto. It is even farther from Earth on average than Pluto is, but it is not as far as Eris. Makemake orbits the sun at a distance of about 4.3 billion miles (6.9 billion km). It takes it about 306 Earth years to complete each orbit. Its orbit is fairly elongated, though not as much

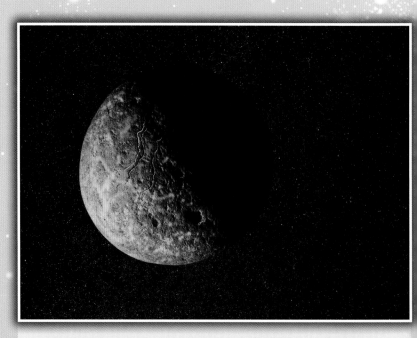

Makemake, shown in this drawing, is named after a creator god in the mythology of Rapa Nui (Easter Island). Makemake was discovered a few days after the Easter holiday.

as Pluto's or Mercury's. Makemake's orbit is also very tilted. Makemake is reddish in color. Its surface is thought to be covered with frozen methane.

Makemake was discovered on March 31, 2005. It was named 2005 FY9 until 2008, when it received an official name and classification. It became the fourth dwarf planet and the third plutoid to be classified. In April 2015, the Hubble Space Telescope first observed a moon orbiting Makemake.

The Hubble Space Telescope first captured an image of Makemake's moon about ten years after the dwarf planet was discovered.

CERES

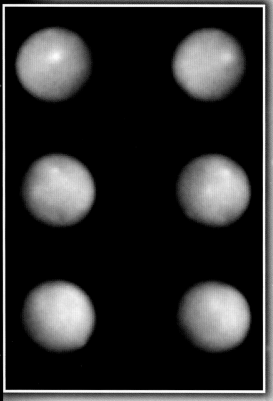

These six images show the rotation of Ceres. It takes 9.1 Earth hours to complete a full rotation.

Ceres is both the largest asteroid and a dwarf planet. It lies within the main asteroid belt. Ceres is sphere-shaped and somewhat flattened at its poles. The diameter at its equator is about 610 miles (980 km), while the diameter at its poles is about 565 miles (910 km).

Ceres is an average of 257 million miles (414 million km) from the sun. It completes one orbit around the sun every 4.6 Earth years. One rotation around its axis, or one day, takes 9.1 hours.

Scientists have found signs that Ceres gives off water vapor from certain areas. This vapor was the first water to be detected in the asteroid belt. Like Earth, Ceres is thought to have three main layers. Scientists believe that it has a rocky core surrounded by a thick, icy mantle and a thin crust.

The brightest spot on Ceres, seen here with another less bright spot, is located in the Occator Crater.

Ceres was the first asteroid to be discovered. Italian astronomer Giuseppi Piazzi spotted it on January 1, 1801. He named it after the ancient Roman goddess of grain. Piazzi originally thought Ceres was a comet. Then it became clear that, unlike a comet, it had a planet-like orbit. At first astronomers considered Ceres and the similar bodies that were later discovered between Mars and Jupiter to be planets. In the mid-1800s, they started calling these bodies asteroids. Ceres was named a dwarf planet in 2006.

In 2007, NASA, the US space agency, launched the unmanned space probe Dawn on a mission to Ceres and another asteroid. Since reaching Ceres'

This sculpture depicts Ceres, who is the goddess of the growth of food crops in Roman mythology.

How is Ceres like other known dwarf planets? How is it different?

orbit in 2015, it has sent back a lot of information and many images. Dawn provided images of a tall mountain called Ahuna Mons and a large crater, the Occator Crater. The images show bright spots in the crater, which could be caused by salts.

The unmanned spacecraft Dawn is shown between a large asteroid named Vesta (*left*) and Ceres in this drawing.

NEW FRONTIERS OF EXPLORATION

Dawn and New Horizons were the first spacecraft to send us information about dwarf planets, but scientists hope they will not be the last. Astronomers believe there could be as many as 100 or more dwarf planets to discover in the Kuiper belt. Outside of it, there could be many more! Sedna and 2012 VP113 are just some of the objects that could be classified as dwarf planets next.

In 2007, scientists discovered an object they called 2007 OR 10. Many scientists think that it should be classified as a dwarf planet.

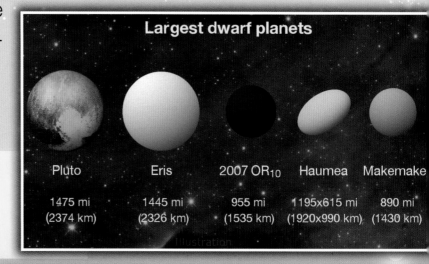

Largest dwarf planets

Pluto	Eris	2007 OR$_{10}$	Haumea	Makemake
1475 mi (2374 km)	1445 mi (2326 km)	955 mi (1535 km)	1195x615 mi (1920x990 km)	890 mi (1430 km)

Illustration

Compare space exploration to exploring unknown regions on Earth. What types of challenges are involved with discovering facts about space?

Although humans have yet to visit dwarf planets, we have already learned a great deal about them. Images of Ceres and Pluto have shown us that, though these distant objects are very different from our world, they still share some qualities with the planets in our solar system. With more exploration, there is no telling what new information we may discover about our solar system and the rest of the universe!

The Kepler Mission (pictured here) continues to search for a space object that humans can live on some day.

GLOSSARY

ASTRONOMER A scientist who studies all of the objects outside of Earth's atmosphere, including the sun, moon, planets, and stars.

AXIS An imaginary straight line passing through the center of a body around which the body rotates.

CHASM A deep hole or opening in the surface of a planet or other body.

CLASSIFICATION Arranging people or things into groups based on ways that they are alike.

COMET A bright heavenly body made up of ice and dust that develops a cloudy tail as it moves closer to the sun in its orbit.

CONTROVERSY Strong disagreement about something among a large group of people.

CRATER A large round hole in the ground made by something falling from the sky.

DETECT To notice something that is hidden or hard to find.

DIAMETER The distance through the center of an object from one side to the other.

EQUATOR An imaginary circle around a heavenly body that is equally distant from the north pole and the south pole at all points.

MANTLE The part of a solid planet that lies beneath the surface and above the center.

MYTHOLOGY The rich collection of traditional tales called myths from cultures all over the world.

ORBIT To travel on a curved path around an object.

POLE Either end of the line passing through a spinning object's center, around which the object spins.

PROBE A device used to send back information, especially from outer space.

ROTATION The act of turning around an axis or central point.

SOLAR SYSTEM A star, such as our sun, along with the group of heavenly bodies that revolve around it, such as planets, moons, asteroids, and comets.

VAPOR A substance in the form of a gas.

FOR MORE INFORMATION

Books

Carson, Mary Kay, and Tom Uhlman. *Mission to Pluto: The First Visit to an Ice Dwarf and the Kuiper Belt*. Boston, MA: Houghton Mifflin Harcourt, 2016.

Kortenkamp, Steve. *Demoting Pluto: The Discovery of the Dwarf Planets*. North Mankato, MN: Capstone Press, 2016.

Portman, Michael. *Why Isn't Pluto a Planet?* New York, NY: Gareth Stevens Publishing, 2013.

Roza, Greg. *Pluto: The Dwarf Planet*. New York, NY: Gareth Stevens Publishing, 2011.

Stewart, Kellie. *Journey to Pluto and Other Dwarf Planets*. New York, NY: Rosen Publishing, 2015.

Websites

Because of the changing nature of internet links, Rosen Publishing has developed an online list of websites related to the subject of this book. This site is updated regularly. Please use this link to access this list:

http://www.rosenlinks.com/PE/pluto

INDEX